"Shareefa is somebody I've seen pe
always been moved by the obvioɪ
Getting the chance to read her words
a new insight into just how beautifu
is and i've been grateful for the oppɪ
qualities of the name Shareefa are compassionate & idealistic, I
think Galaxy Walk proves that she is both of those things
and so much more"

RODNEY P, THE GODFATHER OF UK HIP HOP

"Powerful truthful words straight from the heart. An important
new voice wonderfully and widely engaged with the issues of
our times."

SAMIA MALIK, SINGER

Shareefa Energy is a poet, spoken word artist, writer, and poetry and creative writing workshop facilitator. She is of Indian heritage, from working-class Highfields in Leicester. London has been her home since 2010. She is known for her impactful work in London and beyond as an activist, educator and performer, and has a BA in International Relations.

Her poetry has featured on BBC's *The One Show*, Channel 4 and ITV, and has been published in *i-D* magazine and various publications.

Shareefa performed at Poetry Meets Hip Hop in Berlin and festivals including the Verve Festival and Flamenco Festival. She was headline poet for BBC Radio 1Xtra *Words First* 2019. She received the UK Entertainment Best Poet Award 2017 and was shortlisted for the Eastern Eye Arts, Culture & Theatre Award 2019 by the Arts Council.

She has facilitated creative writing and poetry workshops internationally, from Palestine to Sierra Leone, with children in primary schools and lecturers in universities among others. She was artist in residence at North Kensington Library for the Apples and Snakes Spine Festival 2018 and 2019.

Galaxy Walk

Shareefa Energy

Burning Eye

Burning Eye Books
Never Knowingly Mainstream

Supported using public funding
**ARTS COUNC
ENGLAND**

LOTTERY FUNDED

This edition published by Burning Eye Books 2019

www.burningeye.co.uk
@burningeyebooks

Burning Eye Books
15 West Hill, Portishead, BS20 6LG

ISBN 978-1-911570-78-3

Photography and cover design: RGZGcreative © 2019

Galaxy Walk

Love and blessings Aisla
Master. Thank you for
being an inspiring woman
always standing in your
truth.

XxX

Shereefa.

For those living in the margins

CONTENTS

Life Force Resuscitated   10

PEGASUS CLOSE   13

No Chapatti Like Maa's   14
Silhouette Of An Eagle   16
The Tailors   17
Rusk   18
Mirror, Mirror On The Wall   19
Prodigy   20
Pee-Eye-Gee   22
Eighteen   23
Innit   24

DIASPORA BLUES   25

I Carry You   26
Mama's Dream   29
Thomas Cook   30
Papa's Voyage   32

JURY IN SPACE   35

Rajasthan's Flamenco   36
Sweet Salone   38
Indus Valley   42
Jabal Al-Zaytoun   44
Tired   46
Displaced Development   49
No Tourists   52
Burying Hercules   53
Toy Guns   54

GRENFELL RD   57

Eyewitness Report   58
One Year Later   60
Britain's Minefield   62

KALEIDOSCOPE   65

Heaven's Kitchen   66
Shade   67
Turn Down The Volume   68
Phantasmagoria   70
Submission   72

SEARCHING FOR SHUKRA   75

Seekers Of Protection   76
Men Of God   77
Avalanche   78
Apologies In Braille   79
Has He Learnt To Make Love Yet?   80
That's What He Said   82

LAPIS LAZULI   83

Two Steps Back   84
Nat Mur   85
The Science Of Eight Limbs   86

SATURN RETURN   87

The Hen And The Cockerel   88
Sidewalk   90
She With Scales   91
Yoni Verse   92
Bhaji On The Beach   93
Rebirth   94
Phoenix Rises   96

LIFE FORCE RESUSCITATED

There are times in life when a woman feels her creative energy becomes stagnant. There are intricate thoughts, ideas and truths to be released; her life force depleted, leaving her with little strength and motivation. She sits with gems tucked behind her hair. Waiting to be called upon and freed, gifts to be shared.

When a woman faces predicaments in her life, when her higher self may be in combat, sword in hand, whilst trying to break free from *all* that the lower self is provoked so easily by, she may go into hiding.

Her higher self may not feel nurtured or valued. She may feel overshadowed by realities that speak otherwise. Her wisdom and intuition have the ability to drown confusion, yet her inner voice remains muffled.

She may recite poems or support others with her ability to see situations with acumen, but when she looks into her own life, her pineal gland is paralysed, consumed by her inner struggles.

She may feel her poetry recitals become mere words, whilst still having the capacity to move. She has the drive to honour her gifts, knowing the importance of sharing them with the universe. Even the most fecund apple tree needs water to sustain itself, the most generous home needs love and compassion, hands that wipe tears require being held too. Energy should be exchanged fairly.

Blockages need undoing. Headspace needs creating. Nurturing environments for women to feel safe and appreciated are vital.

A woman needs to focus on lifting the burden of her financial restraints; those close to her may need seeing to before her. She may put away her pen, paintbrush and notebook to tend to another garden. She may forget how much her own garden needs delicate attentive hands to soften the formation of knots. She may feel a tug from the neighbours' falling fence each time she tries to plant her own tomatoes.

A woman who attracts relationships where she feels undervalued or belittled may withdraw, disconnecting from her strengths. As though her nightingale voice that inspires standing ovations is unworthy of love and admiration. She may begin to shy away. She may almost forget, but every so often a hum exits her chest and a poetic line is scrawled into the margins of minutes.

My message is to honour the thin silence of the voice that wants to escape from your mouth and fingertips. Never surrender to metamorphosis into a dehydrated and malnourished mammal, when confronted with the attempted strangulation of spirit.

Speak. Speak like your lungs are gasping for breath. Write. Write in the bathroom if that is the only place you feel safe. Sing when waiting for the train. Pick up the microphone again and reconnect with words written with clarity and grounding. Channel your life force into your creativity.

Speak with conviction, like someone's life is depending on the echo of your words. Speak like desert storms may pause to momentarily listen. Speak like the word is intended to be spoken.

Let the chakra that may have calloused your creative expression unlock like dolphins porpoising for air.

PEGASUS CLOSE

NO CHAPATTI LIKE MAA'S

Wish I could write poetry to my grandmother
in Gujarati. Weave intricate stories
and memories, share acknowledgement
of her, a blessing in my life, illustrate
all histories etched in my story.

Half-term excitement as a child,
logs of books selected at Highfields library,
hidden away tucked into a grocery
bag. Skipping. The waft and aroma
of her cooking in Maa's Kitchen
            – better make it before ten thirty,
gliding my feet down Galaxy Walk,
just in time to eat fresh chapattis.

Mum made rotis too;
there was an extra special taste
of *babi* made by Maa's hands, her delicate
wrinkled hands carving circles before
placing dough onto a *Tawa*:
            wrists flicking, flour inflating,
            palms rotating, chapatti flipping.

Resting elbows on the kitchen
table. Eyes wide, hunger
staring, hands washed, tongue
salivating. Awestruck as she graced
piping round hot chapattis
            onto a flower-decorated plate.
Chair scraping the kitchen floor,
pushing in, about to tuck
in, butter spread by her flour-
glittered hands, chapatti rolled
like ancient scrolls, grandchild
grateful to savour.

Maa's recipe nobody could imitate,
      for the taste lay in the buds
of her fingertips. Her granddaughter

later learnt, in her youth, she birthed chapatti
for whole villages.

Blessed to swallow morsels from Maa's hands,
onions hissing on the stove,
shedding their skin to her flute at the crack of dawn,
gluttonous rituals, three sittings on Eid day:
        in the afternoon, at dinner, when uncles
and cousins came.
Licking fingers, gobbling two lamb biryani
plates, no rice grain visible,
fingers masala-stained.

SILHOUETTE OF AN EAGLE

Scorned for the hair above her lip.
Teased where her eyebrows meet.
Silhouette of an eagle,
markings of a warrior,
etched on her forehead
        in the distance.

THE TAILORS

Sewing, stitching, cutting patterns,
        punching needles into fabric,
foot on pedal
        accelerating, reversing,
pencilling neck shapes onto carbon paper.

        Toddlers left in the sanctuary of Bengali women,
aunties in flamboyant saris,
        lips stained amber,
chewing betel leaves;
        a canary and saffron
rocking horse awaits,
        child magicians circled,
manifested in the Argos catalogue.
        The crèche a palette of Toys 'R' Us.

The Bengali Community Centre
on Melbourne Road,
        seamstresses teaching Mama to sew.
        Wardrobe tailored by tailors,
tailors with tape draped around their nape,
fabrics selected in Buxton Textiles, the Golden Mile
        and Alum Rock Road.

Mama picks me up from the playground,
        crisp packet kicked aside by time,
hurries me back to her sewing class,
        metallic, flourescent thread rolls.
Red Leicester volcano.

The drill of the Brother sewing machine
        a tremor in our home,
metallic, fluorescent thread rolls.

Teenage daughters once uncomfortable,
busts no longer measured by strangers.

RUSK

biscuits
essential in every South Asian diaspora home,
the early nineties.
Baaji would buy a box,
lid transparent,
brick-brown
honeycomb limestone
placed next to a plate
of *jeera* biscuits,
dipped into masala tea.

I never drank tea,
dipped mine into Mum's mug
when she wasn't looking.
Soggy
collapse,
evidence gathered.
Rusk biscuits:
reminiscing
my grandfather,
Baaji.

MIRROR, MIRROR ON THE WALL

who's the fairest?
Indian children chant in *madrassa*,
comparing skin tones,
peering into eyes to glimpse hazel,
pulling out the end of their plaits
from under hijabs.
Eyes wide: *Her hair is brown!*
– fangirling over Snow White.

An Indian mother asked her daughter's friend,
Come over here, let me see who is prettier,
grabbed my wrist to place over her child's.
Both children frowned, stood awkward;
my mother, irritated, praised the scolded girl.

An elderly woman gloats,
Mari nawasi gori na jiwi lageh
(my granddaughter looks like a white girl).
My grandmother raises a brow.

Daughters in India wear socks with sandals:
No one will marry me if my feet are dark,
anxious over potential husbands
inspecting, encumbered by foot
fetish, self-consciously she carries
trays of masala chai and samosas
for suitors.

English women in Indian tailors'
magazines modelling Asian bridal wear
– even the Aishwarya Rais no longer
qualify.

Scars colonialism planted,
potent salt rubbed into wounds,
the caste system reeks putrid.

PRODIGY

I was always proud,
my younger and only brother.
His year 4 teacher, Miss Ipgrave,
she saw his ocean potential
lent this eight-year-old her novels:
Lord of the Rings, Artemis Fowl.

I was three years older academically,
used to look at the thickness,
hopping over them camouflaging
the staircase to find him typing
away with mini fingers,
wandering through galaxies
in orbit, saving copies of his stories
onto floppy discs. By the time
I hit year 9 SATs, my brother
was doing the same English exam
in year six.

I had high aspirations for him.
He wanted to go to the same
secondary school as his friends,
the one I knew would swallow
and leave him parched.
Just another Asian boy.
Knowing they had no faith in these boys,
seeing their minds as inferior
knowing they wouldn't give him
the guidance he needed –
they would insult
his intelligence, throw him
into bottom sets.

I was still too young,
could only grow hysterical
when he was choosing his GCSEs,
an extra GCSE year I did at college
though I had A's,
but *they weren't enough.*

I demanded the college
re-choose his subjects,
knowing his intelligence
he'd forgotten;
the system didn't respect BTEC.
I remember his words
wrapped aroud my throat:
I'm not clever anymore!

I cried
for him not getting the right support,
his mind not being nurtured,
taken from the windowsill
into a dust-ridden cupboard.
We didn't have the privilege
to prise open doors;
he could have been published,
but nobody in my family knew.

PEE-EYE-GEE

Contentedly sat in the canteen,
enthusiastically tucking into my vegetarian meal.

      Hey, is anyone sitting there?
I politely say no.
As their tray begins to level with mine
I breathe in deep, haraam bells: oh no!
Chewing whilst not inhaling,
attempts to block out the lethal smell.

Another two students park their trays next to mine.
My plate is in some serious
                    checkmate.
Don't they know
a Muslim girl's nightmare being surrounded by pork?

      I side-eye my right neighbour:
jerk pork.
      I blink at the opposite tray:
shredded pork.
      Claustrophobia kicks in.

      I look to my left: pork sausages.
Trying not to heave into my plate,
I start wondering what was on my plate before my food.
      The Muslim girl's siren shrieks
red, red, red!

My meal doesn't seem so enticing anymore.
Day after day in the canteen
I must find a secluded spot to eat.

Please don't make me lose my appetite.
Please keep away your haraam meat.
I come from a place where children say *pee-eye-gee*.
Please stay away from my table and let me eat in peace.

Attention, attention, this Muslim is eating.
Please keep that pork away from me.

EIGHTEEN

Birthday arrives. Eighteen days in quick succession. Eighteen. The assumptions. The adrenaline. The unzipping of childhood. Eighteen. A thick coat of adult overnight. The naivety. The inability to take responsibility. Eighteen. The growing pains yet to come. The love that believes it will last. The heartache. Eighteen. The turbulence. The harsh optician's appointment. Rose-tinted spectacles stampeded. Eighteen. Friends who would drift. Self-appointed judges. Eighteen. Those who parents warned not to run around after. Who would soon be nowhere. Eighteen. Planning summer holidays without family. Excited children plot. Giggle. Embracing the portal. Unaware of what awaits.

INNIT

Do you want elocution lessons?
Speak properly! How can someone
who says 'innit' be a poet?
Should have stuck to being a rapper;
they definitely are not poets.

That thick working-class ethnic
dialect gives me a headache,
those Highfields hoodlum Mozlems,
women who speak like 'Innit, bruv!'
They'll never excel in life;

they don't even respect the Queen's English.

DIASPORA BLUES

I CARRY YOU

It's been nine months now / I wear your jumpers / they still carry your scent / if you knew you'd cuss me / tell me to buy my own clothes

Thick hair to your shoulders / your clones in my nightmares / you'd buy me Yorkie bars / I'd hide behind the front room door / throw them at your feet / Maa would tell you to leave

You used to throw me to the stars and catch me / your laugh contagious / your head tossed backwards / you rumbled / I was always proud / linking your arm as we'd walk / strides to keep up / trying not to get hit by your white cane as you'd speed up

We weren't on good terms / Mum's outburst told us the truth / cancer had colonised / my heart was strangled that night

•

I'd visit the oncology ward / sometimes you wouldn't know I was there / my voice parked outside / your lids closed to shadows / stifled / aware sobs from choking on tears would cause you upset

The chemotherapy started / your hair thinned / I stopped coming to see you for a while / creating new memories I couldn't bear / knowing any moment we could lose you / prostate cancer they said / spread to your lungs / four years you soldiered on

Till June 2012 / your sister rang / announced you had a heart attack / I sobbed on the train / you ruffled my pixie cut and laughed hysterical / 'It felt like an elephant was sitting on my chest!' / farewell bid with a beam / 'Make sure you come back for my funeral'

I stood up to leave / a nervous laugh escaped / you'd become invincible / confident decades ahead were written

Few months later in Sierra Leone / Mum rang / her voice low
/ your health had deteriorated / I dismissed how serious /
when I got back / Mum called again

You looked fragile / didn't like the killer bees in your wheeze
/ told you I'd only come home to see you / you agreed to let
me stay

Three nights / a sleeping bag / the floor next to your bed /
you'd cough and wake / Farley would sit up from her basket
/ I'd switch on your oxygen / pass you the mask / anxious till
your breath returned to a steady pace

Strength vacuumed / stairs muscle memory / thoughts
went through your head / no children / wanting to share /
encouraging me to enjoy the jet shower now useless / dawning
on how your loss would affect me / whispered to ask if I'd
eaten / you could hardly swallow or stomach soup

You asked what I learnt in Sierra Leone / your perspective still
healthy / 'We are lucky, you know'

 Mum told me to hug you / bye / couldn't bring myself to /
I squeezed your hand / said I'd be back Friday / you nodded
/ *don't trouble yourself* / placed my palm on your head / we
both knew this could be the last time we saw each other / with
breath still in your lungs

Thursday night / sat in the university café sharing anecdotes
/ had missed a call from my mum / a text came from a far
relative / *I'm really sorry Shareefa* / didn't know how to react /
my temper kicked in / news digesting / tears began to stream
/ the whole family was with you / except me / Maa's hands
on her child's difficult cheeks / trying to wake you / she
shattered

Refused painkillers / wanted to be awake when the hour closed / you smiled / like to believe you caught a glimpse of Maa / for the first and last time

•

Wish I'd spent more time with you / been better / miss calling you every time I see a trampoline / laughing as we recollect 'Miss Trunchbull' jumping with me / wish we took you to Farm World / not as if you hadn't asked since I was a kid / I recall you bought me a hamster / distraught we'd never met / joked it smelt worse than your dog / my dad made you return to the pet shop

I saw us losing you / still smoking roll-ups / after you passed / I withdrew / picked up a draw / it became a part of my life / rain in fog / I leave the grocer's with bars of Aero mint / chocolate bubbles you'd gift me

I love you *Gurrah Mama* / wish we'd travelled / wish you got to visit your grandfather's bungalow in India / 'Iqbal *Manzil*' / Iqbal Palace / after you / you're still here / Eid's never been the same / you never had children / a father to me

MAMA'S DREAM

Mama wants us
to go on holiday,
one big happy.

Haven't been on a plane
       together
since I was ten.

Mama wants
us to go on holiday,
play one big happy.

How do I tell her
times have changed,
we've all aged.

The eldest has her
own to entertain.
We all have separate lives;

they don't intertwine.
Your children aren't close,
Mama, it's too late.

THOMAS COOK

I see the beauty
through the flames of the hell.
I know my test is to be mentally
and spiritually strong,
though they try to entrap people physically,
a psychological bully.

I know I've got to strengthen my spirit
in preparation for dark times;
only live once on this Earth
in our lifeline.
I'm not blind to the reality
and negative energies they boil.

I stay awake sewing together
my spiritual shield.
So many spirits they're disturbing.
Me they are not fooling;
stalling, I see the truth
even when I take a breather.

Truth can be overwhelming.
I'd rather feel truth
than continue to believe
the way they present the world
to be a Thomas Cook magazine.

Sunhats, tans, brown sand and sunscreen.
Cycling around on our holidays
not knowing in Australia
there was a mass grave,
Rottnest Island concentration camp.

They only tell us what they need to get tourism stamps.
So many lies they've told, I don't buy it.
I've been to Toronto, no mention of the indigenous man.
When I went to France to see Disneyland,
only a teenager, posed for pictures with an army man.

If school had showed me in their history plan
the truth of France's plunder,
their bloody hands,
if school had shown me *The Battle of Algiers*
I would have been more astute than an army fan.

They glossed over Europe's colonial past,
made me feel wrongly frustrated in my history class.
Always knew something wasn't right,
didn't buy the story of being simply an economic migrant's child.
A confused diaspora, stuck in a trio of identities,

Muslim, British, Indian,
pulled in different directions like curious elasticity.
Where do I go / Who am I / Where am I supposed to be
They made me feel inferior,
I billowed my A's in their faces from my GCSEs.

I come from a great culture of old civilisations
and the literate.
Poetry's in my veins,
in the melody of my father's old Hindi cassettes.
I choose to express and not let the fire burn in my chest.

I set my paper alight with my pen,
notebook and microphone my closest friends.
History's ongoing; it doesn't stay in the past tense.
They're denying Caribbean islands reparations;
there's no blur in my history lens.

Tell Thomas Cook to cook up a new tourism guide,
not one to ogle at the indigenous but with truth to confide.
I don't want to be blind like the shock on a tourist's face,
when witnessing sleeping bags in Victoria
expecting only shopping and daisies.

PAPA'S VOYAGE

Stereotypes of Muslim fathers –
oppressive, aggressive.
If it wasn't for my father
I wouldn't be where God willed me to be.

He gave my wings a sky to spread beneath,
to soar, to believe, to achieve,
be a master, succeed,
push boundaries,
travel, expand my mind.
He learnt to understand, accept,
the spirit of his last daughter.

I often wonder what my father's dreams
were before England, aged seventeen.
How he envisaged bringing up children
away from the villages in Gujarat
where buffalos graze,
fresh milk each morning, hot from their udders,
mouth-watering mango, custard apple trees,
nostalgic aromas,
his mother's cuisine,
fresh coriander drizzled on *khuri kitchari*.

Leaving luminous stars from moonlit nights
for grey skies and the polluted English city,
decades of sweat in Leicester's textile factories,
a care worker in his fifties,
always making sure there was food on our plates.

I wonder what he thought his children would be like.
At times we used to argue and fight,
a father adjusting to his daughter no longer a child.

I have the fire of my father,
his mascara concerned eyes,
his love often difficult to communicate.
I am proud to be his daughter,
a strand of silk from his silver beard.

JURY IN SPACE

RAJASTHAN'S FLAMENCO

Hooves against the wet pavement,
rhythmic patterns
heel to toe, toe to heel,
pearl droplets of rain,
an echoing cacophony.

A man sat in the shadows
strumming his string sitar,
wooden pipe clenched between his teeth,
a visible oar from the corner of his mouth,
moustache and cotton shirt dampened,
eyelashes tightly embraced.

The jewels around her ankles gliding,
sticking to her skin at intervals,
blood skirt flowing,
dancing as she moves,
hypnotic hips twisting,
blouse cupping her perfect bosom,
sharp collarbones displayed,
ruffles caressing her as she glides,
pivoting into a frenzy.

She was the mother,
the teacher,
glossy hair stuck to her cheeks,
the royal gold of her bangles,
smudges of kohl around her eyes,
almond rain glistening on her midriff.

The queen of the Rajas.
They called her *gypsy*, derogatory.
Footprints sighted in Iran, Iraq,
Turkey, generations would travel
from India, Rajasthan and Punjab,
dancing for bread and butter.

Her spirit mimicked,
Moorish influence merges
paraded on pavements
of Al-Andalus and Granada.

The riffs of the guitar,
callings of the sarangi,
drumming of the dholak's *dhaap*,
tapping of the flamenco's feet,
bells of the kartal,
vocals of the *jugalbandhi*
intertwined with its twin,
the familiarity of the taal,
the twelve-beat rhythm of the flamenco bulería,
wooden shoes and the Ghunghroo *chum chum.*

Waterfalls flow in her smile,
her playfulness exudes as she dances.
Dramatic tugs and jerks
of the flamenco's intensity,
both spines straight.

SWEET SALONE

Sierra Leone, she never gets to catch her breath.
Had every intention to revisit,
but when Mama Teda died
what was the point of going back
to Kono?

Who would I sit beside to listen to the radio?
Cook eggs with love and avocado?
Who would I run to when the girls were in trouble?
Who would cry out *'eh-bo!'* in response to a happening?

I'd return to the compound, on tiptoes,
sandals in hand from the diamond mine,
trying not to get the floor dirty,
diarrhoea mud up to my knees,
assisting local men digging and sieving
who wanted independence
from foreign mining companies.
The beautiful frail elder
who'd treat me like I was his granddaughter,
he'd help pour water, I'd exfoliate
my legs, the dirt on my feet disolved.
What happened to him?

And what about Patrick?
Who said if men and women were equal
then women would surely climb coconut trees
to bring down gourds.

I wept when Matthew Swarray died,
my treasured friend who crashed his motorbike.
I recall his laughter
making the engine go faster,
holding on for life,
wheels hitting potholes.
One night the fuel ran out,
sat in the dark, rain pouring,
waiting for a headlight from a passer-by.

What about Muhammad James the tailor,
hair in thick locs, my Muslim brother?
He introduced me to Kono's storytellers,
took me to brothels and clubs
to support women –
a watcher hawk.

What about social worker Jason?
Amused every time I'd yell *Jheez!*
Pelting through the market
on the compound motorbike,
confused: *Why you saying Jesus?*

                                        Say Muhammad.

What about the professor?
The encyclopaedia
who gave me history lessons
late at night, from Britain to Freetown.

What about the pleasant woman?
Her daughter's voice lathered
in honey, the one who gifted me
pepper fish, emptying her purse.
Burning my stomach,
heard I was Indian and added
too much chilli.

What about Fatima?
The fiery model
who wouldn't accept nonsense,
who shared her blessings with struggling women,
opening her home.

What about Black Diamond?
Mama Teda warned me was a nuisance,
the too-familiar look in his eyes.
He grew up in Holland and Croydon
before repatriating.

What about T-Boy?
Evenings we'd sit on the veranda
insisting on stories, lightning-flash
street lights, turning me into a grandmother
before my time. Discussing racism
in Britain, shifting his perspective;
he learnt white girls
have teenage pregnancies too.
Did he go to school in the end?
Did he reach his full potential?
Did he get off the streets, go back
to living with his mum?
A blessed child, so much affection,
a painful farewell when leaving Kono.

What about Khadiatou? Lucia?
What happened to my little sisters?
The playful aunties, women in villages
who would greet me with teases:
Small small pikin, but she read book!

What happened to the compassionate boys,
the vendors who sold drinks on street corners,
passionate about foreigners not taking from their land,
        concerned over the wellbeing of their young sisters;
*If Salone got money for our resources,
our sisters wouldn't be on the streets;
they would be the next First Lady!*
        – the boys with bright eyes.

When I heard news of Ebola,
when mudslides crushed over five hundred lives,
my Salone family remained in the forefront of my mind.

This flood, this mudslide,
this quick mud,
this mud holding bodies.

INDUS VALLEY

Attempts to untangle from the mesh
the complication of identity.
Nothing appears simplistic;
Indian diaspora Muslim youth.

Many tangents, branches,
stories, advances,
many collisions, chances,
our intermittence between classes
seemingly casteless,
every nook and cranny magnified,
attempts to hide our initial liberation,
reflected in statues of young girls
from the Indus valley.

Our figures, our breasts,
experiences hidden in the cleavage
of our chest,
gasping for breath,
fastening our saris in elastic,
interwoven in our glossy silk fabric
before the British came,
horrified by our expression,
sexualising us, Orientalists giving us blouses.

Maa sat at her teak table grinding spices,
indigenous, life still breathing,
a reflection of my ancestors
in hidden away non-gentrified villages,
authentic.

Billowing voices that never escaped ribcages,
even in ghettoised communities in Western society.
Learning to embrace myself as a woman,
an Indian queen,

The power of my ancestors comes from Indian,
not Arab Muslim land.
If my blood is mixed with Arabs and Persians
when the Moghuls came,
am I of a pure traceable route?
Am I simply what they told me and I claimed?
Am I of Burmese origin if Mama was born on Burmese land?
Pure economics when Britain colonised
and took over our land,
neo-colonialism's nails dug deep,
yet I live on a foreign land.

My eyes are open.
Cannot self-identify through one lens alone.
My spirit speaks, my soul journeys.
I am from another space, another time.
My ancestors speak boldly through my bloodline.

JABAL AL-ZAYTOUN

Wish I could take you to Jerusalem with me.
To Haifa, to witness sand,
                              water fountains, the sea.

Walk past the border,
no checkpoints, no illegal stop and search
by European teenagers this land does not belong.

Wish I could take you to Jerusalem with me,
walk amongst your rich history and olive trees,
leave fingerprints on Al-Aqsa and the Dome of the Rock.

Pace your land freely,
splash water where Muslims perform ablution,
bow down and prostrate with the sun on your nape,

stroll through the Old City and Damascus Gate,
wander the city's cobbled streets,
hydrate with homemade lemonade at afternoon break.

No hostile settlers paranoid
when crossing the four quarters,
armies of scrawny alley cats taking over.

Wish I could take you to Jerusalem with me,
plant tomato seeds by your ancestors' graves,
picturesque postcard landscape from the Mount of Olives,

feed your eyes vivid images,
no necessity to translate from poetry,
nostrils singed overwhelmed with freedom's scent.

Mahmoud Darwish's poetry in graffiti,
hip-hop on Jerusalem's streets,
the *Adhaan* the cockerel waking the city

I am sorry it was I
who got to witness more of your land,
privilege in a British passport.

TIRED

with this world,
the trauma of this.
Tired of Gaza being bombed,
friends restless to hear from
family to see if they're still alive,
of hearing the most morbid stories
of survivors of genocide.

Tired of attending protests
and only being able to raise a flag,
shaking with tears outside embassies,
the grieving of thousands of lives
being more than overwhelming.

Tired of seeing children lose their parents
to the bullets of police in the UK and the US.
Tired of seeing sisters who want to hug
their brother again, mothers whose daughters
will never give them grandchildren,
fathers and sons who never got to express
their love to each other, women who sleep
beside cold pillows, their lovers who'll
never return.

Tired of parents burying their just-learnt-to-walk-and-talk
    children,
of seeing fellow communities mourning,
of the inferiority complex of western liberal democracies
bombing and obliterating histories and libraries,
pointing fingers as though ISIS are the only barbarians
to have chopped off people's heads.

Tired of having to mobilise, the spiritual war
with ugly spirits running the globe isn't over yet.
Tired of silent heartbeats making elites a bag of money.
Tired of the number of people traumatised imprisoned
multiplying,
returning home with scars after decades in Guantanamo Bay.

Tired of refugees' makeshift homes labelled as jungles,
voices in detention centres strangled and silenced.
Tired of the pretence of racism being a new reality for migrants.
Tired of Muslim graves being desecrated by BNP, UKIP,
swastikas drawn on with poison.

Tired of Muslim children taught in schools,
'Muslims kill,' and African children taught
their only history is slavery – how empowering.

Tired of explaining resistance and demands for dignity
of the wretched of the Earth to feel-good advocates
of 'non-violence', all-day every-day liberals,
assuming charity is enough,
hesitant to support self-determination and liberation.

Tired of witnessing glee in the eyes of settlers
who celebrate with fireworks when
an indigenous family in the land they have occupied
has been singed to death by one of them.

Tired of feeling paralysed at times when
news reaches and senses are heightened
– waking like we're all in funeral homes.

Tired of knowing truths I'm not able to comprehend.
Tired of seeing people hurting around me.
Tired of knowing I'm far from the only one that's hurting.
Tired of white supremacy and colonialism that never ended.
Tired of the war machine,
of Chilcot or not, so many inquests but still no justice.

Tired of seeing pain in the faces of families
haunted by the brutal loss of loved ones.
Tired of smiles being snatched from faces,
hearing news of another one.

Tired of feeling desensitised at times,
knowing I shouldn't always tune in
for my own peace of mind,
feeling there's infinite suffering.

Tired of privileged pretending,
going back to business,
till one life is taken for every thousand.

Tired of no-context commentaries when
occupied restless people choose to resist.
Tired of the actions of the oppressed under scrutiny,
coming from mouths not affected by racist police,
no experience of living under military.

Tired of *peace and love* slogans
before justice and equality.
Tired of imagining what this world will be like for my children,
and their children's children.
Tired of wondering whether we've done enough.
Tired of only being able to write
words.

DISPLACED DEVELOPMENT

Notice orders from foreign investors
landing on disgruntled doorsteps,
undisputable time frames distributed,
soil below windowsills uprooted,

mud spluttering, squelching like quicksand,
foreigners posing to 'redevelop' countries after war,
pretences of supporting the mourning,
their eyes gleaming with a moneymaking plan.

NGOs aided by mining companies
one big surreptitious moneymaking scam:
six billion dollars donated for Haiti,
six houses built, two toilets.

Where did the money go for Grenfell – Red Cross?
No transparency or accountability.
Locals in Sierra Leone have to have a licence
to generate an income from diamonds

deep within their own sand.
Pittances paid,
safari suits, chino pockets getting thicker by the band;
they indoctrinate perspectives.

Drastically changes when you land,
blame compliance on local government
shift responsibility from their own hands,
silent about middle-aged white men,

teenage girls in their hotel bed sheets and compound,
sexual misconduct allegations against Oxfam.
They went to *Save the Children;*
children went home empty handed,

tattered garments.
By proxy enforcers slip notices through
gaps under doorways,
adamant heels dug deep resisting

threats to be displaced,
constant battles with the deluded,
reluctantly strapping on orange jackets,
blistering labour, pennies handed.

Manufacturing explosions in mines,
volcano moulded,
the ground trembles;
cement in newly made homes cracks.

No vegetation,
no daily market,
no pleasantries on the compound,
an English-only fools and horses.

Expectations of receiving applause.
She wants to stay living in the jungle
even after being bit by a snake in Mumbai;
the only snake feared has eyes

human-clouded,
resembling those who decades earlier
looted turmeric and cotton.
Future prospects and living arrangements

seemingly uncertain,
remaining defiant, clairvoyant
for born and unborn grandchildren,
children resilient for their parents.

Existence is resistance,
humans should not be at risk of extinction,
brutalised by hungry corporations.
Taxpayers persecuted,

they want to stay home,
continue living in their familiar houses,
no high alert over shoulders,
anxious of elastic pulled out their trousers.

Those who appeared like the village needed saviours,
like the village needed foreigners cringing at soiled feet.

Parading in their neo-colonial boots,
deceiving developers displacing communities in suits.

NO TOURISTS

In our village
the only 'tourists' are familiar faces
resembling previous tenants,
diaspora children,
parents morphing into their tour guide.

Your grandfather was born here,
my uncle built this school
I used to get a rickshaw to this park
buy bhel puri from a street vendor on a Friday,
        the call to prayer trumpets.

There are no tourists in our village.
Extended branches return with English-speaking tongues,
dialects English, some Canadian,
some pull sour faces,
some ecstatic to trace their mother's footprints.

There are no tourists in our village.
Just grandchildren gathered from afar,
admiring their grandmother's face.

BURYING HERCULES

Greek gods beckoned
each time we pronounce names of planets,
yet to reclaim, decolonise,
dethrone.

TOY GUNS

A twelve-year-old boy was shot dead.

A twelve-year-old boy held a toy gun.
Tamir Rice, twelve years old,
only just started secondary school.
Why was he holding a toy gun in the first place?

I saw a child once
walking into the masjid in Hebron
in occupied Palestine
holding a toy gun,
was confused for a moment,
but weren't soldiers
who searched aggressively
on entry all holding

                    real guns?
Didn't the settler innocently
approached to converse with
hold up his

                    real gun?
Weren't settlers casually
on street corners holding

                    real guns?
                    Real guns
as though straps on their shoulders
were just string gym bags
but they were

                    real guns.

Wasn't the state
Tamir Rice was in
occupied by a uniform holding

                    real guns?
Didn't a

                    real gun
shoot and kill him?

How many times will we have to provide
evidence of a sixty-six-year-old white woman

holding up
                    a gun
outside a police station
threatening to shoot
but not being deemed a threat or a terrorist?

How many times will parents
cry over their murdered, non-white
children slaughtered by the state?

What world am I living in?
Was this the destiny of Earth?
Does Jupiter or Neptune hold more compassion?
How many more children will be executed?
How many?
How many women?
How many men?
          Always perceived less important in war,
their trauma brushed to the side,
NGOs advocating for women and children only.
Are men not affected by violence they see?
Is it only daughters who cry when witnessing violence from
    Daddy?
When will there be justice?
When will there be peace?

Oh, Allah,
I ask for pain to be reduced in the hearts of those
who mourn their deceased.

GRENFELL RD

EYEWITNESS REPORT

14th June 2017   11.30am

processing all witnessed since early hours
this morning / local block of flats inflamed and
burning / the screams of grown men and children
/ men waving clothes from windows / rubble and
debris spinning through the sky / falling like
dead crows / processing what this means for the
local community / what it means for the child I
consoled by my side whilst he breathed through
an oxygen mask / for the fathers in soaked
clothes from the hose / in shock not wanting to
register losing their children / men in tears
for losing their wives / people frantic as to
whether they would see again their child / a
woman struggling to breathe / growing hysterical
when receiving news of her husband she couldn't
find / men with cuts on their feet / the force
of falling with hundreds pushing for their life
/ holding the wave down / be strong don't get
emotional now / the trauma of seeing a blazing
building / hours later a giant rotting corpse
/ police trying to move us / friends arriving
with blankets / removing clothes off the drenched
and quivering / praying / hoping the elder who
wants me to meet his wife / praying we hear news
she is still alive / an hour's sleep after being
on the street from 3 am / waking up drenched
in sweat / shaking in uncontrollable sobs /
wondering how deeply my local community who
witnessed / currently on the streets will feel
this / typing with shaking hands / how long will
this trauma grip / what will the funerals look
like / how is this community to recover from the
truth of hearing people screaming / before being
burnt alive / faces flashing before me / bodies
brought out on stretchers / assisting paramedics
/ handing out water and foil blankets / all in
disbelief knowing the

reasons behind the fire expanding / knowing the planners and council don't care for the lives in the flats / easy targets / no sign of a powerful hose to put out the fire / a bigger spray of water only seen hours later / praying those affected are able to recover / sending love and healing to all in close relation / to Grenfell Tower

ONE YEAR LATER

Many tears have fallen since that nightmare of a night
entire families
    left the face of this Earth,
fathers lost their wives and children,
        beautiful children were made orphans.

Over seventy lives lost in an avoidable pre-warned flammable.
Eighteen children accounted for died in their own home,
eighteen bright lights that no longer breathe life.

Did they tell you the aftermath feels like remnants
                         of a war zone?

PTSD on our streets, therapy centre registers almost full,
the tower visible for miles,
a 360-degree constant reminder.

Will our community ever truly recover
                    from this trauma?

A crime scene a year on, tower only partially covered.
Did they tell you how many wake in the morning
to close their blinds?
Haunted by memories of neighbours
crying out for mercy before they died.

How many can see the remains of the tower
from their windows
and on their walk home every day outside?
When the place we're supposed to feel safest is in our home.

Did they tell you how the community pulled together?
Families and neighbours comforting each other,
    one year later
standing together through the inquiry.
Children healing together,
        men and boys able to show emotion.
My heart bleeds for the gaping hole
                of pain left in our community.

One year later:
hundreds are restless,
heartbroken, distressed, pacing,
    from London to Eritrea,
    Egypt, Morocco, Colombia,
waiting for a verdict;
for families' heartfelt tributes to loved ones
                    to not be in vain.

Still waiting for survivors and neighbours to be housed,
for cladding to be removed
    from hundreds of buildings,
for arrests and charges to be pressed,
for those responsible
              to stand in court.

BRITAIN'S MINEFIELD

Flammable cladding in Britain
                                    a time bomb
waiting to explode
                                    anxious eyes dart back and forth
cautious feet on a minefield
                        hundreds fighting with their might to detonate
residents pacing up and down on their blocks
                                    night wardens on shifts
alert neighbours before it's too late
                                    children afraid
'Mummy, is it going to be us next?
        Are we the next Grenfell?'

Mothers forced to lie to their children
                kissing them goodnight
                        tucking them into bed
leaseholders reasonably stressed

                                    building regulations
                began to be questioned
can't ever say Grenfell, Barking or Worcester Park wasn't pre-warned

                        Hundreds of buildings up and down the country
parents dropping their children to schools concerned
                visiting relatives on the oncology ward
                                    looking out their bedside window
                        hearts dropping
recognising the cladding on Grenfell covering
                the hospital's walls.

Voices once hoarse
                                from inhaling thick smoke
bellowing to be heard
                a visible defiant demand projected onto Parliament
                        pressure cannot be ignored
demanding for sprinklers in homes
                        the removal of dangerous flammable cladding
the installing of fire-safe doors.

Hundreds of buildings in Britain wrapped in a time bomb
                residents' demands they attempt to ignore
                        the time bomb is ticking

the state closing their blinds
                    complicit in this terrorism.

So many names responsible
                            when will they be held accountable
          cutting corners
                    lives more important than buildings being
          aesthetically appealing
Grenfell Tower to many was their palace
          an eyesore to Rock Feilding-Mellen, Paget-Brown and
their cronies.

          Hundreds of time bombs ticking
Parliament demanded to listen
          only some feet cautious on Britain's minefield.

                    We Will Never Forget.

                    Seems they have forgotten
they will be reminded
                    again and again
          by residents living in tower blocks
                            by precious souls who lived in Grenfell
by those who survived
                    by families who lost loved ones.

When you remember Grenfell
                            the residents who lived there
remember their strength and resilience
          hope for thousands in times of despair
                    seventy-two lives stolen
                    eighteen of these angels were children
demands will continue
                    for lives to be seen of value
          for children up and down the country
                            for those living in a time bomb
Celotex, cladding companies
          signatories responsible will be held accountable.

Seventy-two lives lost in Grenfell.

                    We Will Never Forget.

KALEIDOSCOPE

HEAVEN'S KITCHEN

papaya   paprika   pomegranate
bell peppers: lemon   chilli   spinach
        chickpeas covered in coconut cream
black seeds   coriander garnish
        roasted aubergine and courgette
                                bejewelled in fresh thyme
        sweet potato straight out the oven
garlic fried mushrooms
                caramelised onions
                        balsamic vinegar drizzled
sliced lady fingers
        cooked-just-right okra
                        experiments with jackfruit
something sweet
something sour
        lemon squeezed on top   couscous
                ackee substitutes eggs for breakfast
        Medjoul dates
blueberries   cacao nibs   flaxseeds
        guava instead of apples
                                meat-cleaver-sliced pineapple
                cinnamon confetti
freshly picked mint tea, Berber whisky
        ginger and turmeric root simmering

                                over ripe mangoes.

SHADE

when journeying through the Amazon rainforest,
ancient trees shield from a sweltering sun
beating down on open pathways,
lava rock mountains.

Trees offer shade by the riverbank,
gliding across sherbet pink sand,
glorious shades of leaves
infusing senses with life when eyes meet.

Shade when lunging uphill,
the gentle breeze as it fans its feathers
welcoming tranquillity in fierce desert heat,
where mothers have stopped to breastfeed.

Shade of trees,
God's mercy,
nature's compassion,
the forest's bounty,
trunks helping limbs
when needing strength,
spine to grip and carry self.

Comforting vineyard roots
gripping a shoe,
guardians when a foot is loose.

Shade of trees,
branches resist order,
grow in circular structures,
portals marking chapters:
You are now on to the next level.

The shelter of trees,
the sun at its peak.
How glorious is the shade?

TURN DOWN THE VOLUME

My inner child is frustrated
with being contained,
forced into a cage,
expected to behave,
        to turn her volume down,
for these English streets
do not hold space for big spirits.

Turn the volume down on your bass,
don't let us hear the treble in your element,
we will strangle the pitch of your soprano.
Happiness of high volumes   is not welcome on this side
    of the bay.

My inner child is frustrated,
wants to swing open patio doors,
run out onto the street with bare feet,
feel the sun ecstatic to greet her skin,
untangling her hairs, the gentle breeze.

My inner child wants to wake daily,
a permanent smile etched on her face,
gradually rocking herself out of her hammock,
stretching, muscles tensing, before greeting the day.

My inner child, she loves to play,
rejoicing freely outside, nature filling her eyes,
hikes through the jungle to bathe in the river.

My inner child wants to throw her head back,
she wants to freeze in her frame,
abs sore, laughter's harmonies giving her bellyache,
deep soul-shaking contagious belly laughs.

My inner child has felt happiness,
visited internal spaces missed out on during childhood,
marvels she could only dream of,
swinging on vine swings just like *The Jungle Book*,
splashing friends, relishing water on her palms.

The frustrations of childhood were straightened out,
memories of staring out the window,
chin in hand attached to a resting elbow,
miserable skies,
the creaking of Mum straightening creases on the ironing board,
wanting to go out, but *right now isn't playtime;*
go read a book!

There were countless travels sitting in Mum's wardrobe,
reading by dolphin torchlight,
Narnia, Peter Pan, Alice in Wonderland,
a sailor between lines,
rocketed to another world,
a meditation pro.

My inner child through the eyes of an adult
saw many delights
more breathtaking than any Kinder Surprise;
the jungle expanded her lungs,
                           let her breathe,
no expectation of quietening down
'cause the adults are trying to sleep.

The Amazon fed her doses of magic
she'd been waiting for,
generous life-resuscitating portions,
jungle pancakes and giant avocado
she ate to her heart's content,
rejoiced till her body stated it was time for bed,
blessed moments captured in her head.

She's back in the concrete
holding on to her free
memories of volumes of happiness,
the score of how her spirit should feel.

PHANTASMAGORIA

Mesmerised.

Spectator transfixed,

    staring at the sky,

        thousands of feathers

           magnetised.

    No firework display could compare,

        nature forming majestic shapes,

                fabricating

           distance, colliding,

           movement observed,

        close bachata, bees orbiting their hive.

Waltzing low,

        gravity draws them close,

    winged stars in the sky,

arrows shooting in unison.

No water breaks.

    Kizomba to the pier,

      left to right,

      vertical to horizontal,

        dot to dot,

          uniform somersaults,

        seconds later barely visible.

        Flamenco theatre from the seashore:

      enchanting choreography a must-see,

  celestial bodies by the sea.

Each wave a sequel to a story,

    clasping treasures and mysteries,

turquoise and bottle green merge intimately.
Beaks peck stones,
webbed feet surf across pebbles,
rotating necks to catch a glimpse of food.

The sea speaks in volumes,
vastness draws in an inquisitive mind,
spirits cleanse
inhaling fresh air by the coastline,
a musical kaleidoscope combined.

Starlings chirp,

the sea gasps,
motion not for the faint-hearted.

Do parts of the sea ever die?

SUBMISSION

Oh you who Believe,
what does it mean to submit?
To submit with pure assurance,
no need for reassurance.

Oh you who Believe,
what does it mean to submit?
I am a Muslim
through my submission
and trust in the Oneness that is God.

Oh you who Believe,
what does it mean to have faith?
Trusting the will of The Most High,
no longer stubborn when seeing signs,
pendulums or *istikhara*
seeking guidance from divinity.

Oh you who Believe,
will you take responsibility when
The Most High responds to your prayer,
to your call?
God said, *Oh you who Believe,*
walk towards me and I will run to you.

I communicate with the creator,
the divine power, the divine force,
the epitome of Love,
the Responsible One, the accountable,
the symbolic language of the universe,
flowing and rippling.
The voice of my intuition,
paying attention to my dreams.

Oh you who Believe,
will you choose to respond
or ignore when God shows up in your life?
Takes your turbulence to safe plains.

The Most High surrounds me with Love,
love of best interest,
acknowledging and embracing me.

I walk with The Most High having my back,
protecting me,
loving me,
blessing me.
I love The Most High for
The Most High is patient with me.
Humans may throw in the towel;
The Most High picks up the pieces,
puts me back together,
makes me whole again.

Oh you who Believe,
what does your submission look like?
Do you truly Believe?

SEARCHING FOR SHUKRA

SEEKERS OF PROTECTION

If I explained the scent of sweat,
the charcoaled walls,
beaten mattresses on floorboards.
If the image wasn't enough,
curious, she would want to see for herself,
from the two camera lenses above her cheekbones.

They say we can hear the whispers
of women before us,
our elder sisters,
guiding us open,
mouths moving but the cries faint.
Attempting to interpret the silhouette
of their mouths before facing predators.

I wonder what realities I've glamorised
in the hope of raising awareness,
admired by a sadist,
a man willing to learn all the tricks
to understand her when she is most vulnerable
for him to be a better hunter.

I wonder if I'm guilty
of pulling off her white robes,
or was that shake needed,
a warning to prevent her from burning?

MEN OF GOD

Some say they are men of God,
yet they teach their women
to doubt their intuition,
place falsehood on divine communication,
drowning out God's voice.

AVALANCHE

When he says the words,
I don't want this anymore,
an avalanche hits my head.
I breathe in, trying to catch my breath,
gut-wrenched, rock snow shards javelin towards me.

Overwhelmed and rejected,
anxious and scared,
replaying flashbacks of being forced to let go,
pushed down the zip wire shrieking,
I'm not ready yet!

The ghosts of my past,
once familiar, now strangers,
barely an acknowledgement.
Hips once locked, tongues nourishing lips parched,
catching each other's breath.

Pleading to be serene inside,
assuming peace has been unearthed
till snow starts to shift again,
mountains begin to crumble,
stifling a scream,
snowboarding at speed,
seeking shelter.

Wondering if some will always
be left at the bus stop,
seeing once-lovers drive by
with their bride.

When he says,
I don't want this anymore,
premonitions of distance fill my periphery,
morphing into a ghost
that forever haunts.

APOLOGIES IN BRAILLE

The instrument in my throat
choked, my voice silent,
I hope you can see the sorry,
the pressure of my lips
                    against yours.

Can your skin read my braille?
Nesting my head in the pit
of your arm. Stroking your fragility,
applying myself
                    again.

Tried to hold on to my bow,
        not speak, protect your clingfilm-wrapped ego.

                You slammed arrows into my palm.
                            I nurse truth's wound.

HAS HE LEARNT TO MAKE LOVE YET?

She wonders if he ever met anyone with the patience
to teach him, his love didn't need to be shown
by digging nails and biting teeth,
by leaving skin broken on the tip of a nipple.

Not understanding all forms of touch
do not equate to affection,
a woman may want to hold and kiss you
        but still say *no*,
he spat out what it means.

Recognising the distance in his eyes
scarred from war, orders received
once by terrified child soldiers,
his experience of intimacy
to only occur with women
who are sex workers,
women deserving –
the most sacred.

Whilst sleeping with women
who desired him,
        no expenses,
he'd lost all sense of innocence,
        of young men learning to touch,
        of young men learning to stroke a cheek
without feeling the need to shove their tongue
between gaps in closed teeth.

She remembers hot tears
falling, eyes that cried
from having to explain
not wanting to go further.
Only desired minimal intimacy,
a burdensome encounter.

Wondering if he learnt to be soft
with his touch, if men thought
aggression was sexy, ever learnt

to make love. No suggestion
that only those labelled as savages
with brown lips face this ordeal.

There are men with white skin
who hyper-sexualise women,
they've continued to move their hips
when a woman's laid limp;
she counts seconds into minutes,
impatient for his mission to end.

How many have penetrated
unaroused women?
Who aren't ready yet,
        need more than sexual frustration,
who need to be listened to under heavy breaths.

A woman who worked for a man
but now she's tired.
Women who deserve more
than death threats,
who deserve autonomy,
who deserve to hold a man without him
        twitching to get his stick in.
Women who are deserving.

Men deserve to experience
a softer world.
A world that says
it's okay to feel butterflies
when mouths collide with butter lips.
Where men are not desensitised,
        unafraid of locking fingers,
stroking palms in admiration like excited children.

Where love is the goal.
Where selfish lust takes a back seat.
When men have learnt to respect
boundaries.

THAT'S WHAT HE SAID

Used to make gods of men,
infatuated, placed them on a pedestal,
now struggles to connect.

Slowly found herself withdrawing,
recoiling, connections proven to be seasonal,
demisexual unimpressed,
adapting to the art of temporary temperaments,
skilful adjustment, a student of the art of detachment,
those she ever loved were never ready to receive her
– some were too late.

Don't get attached, he'd say.
His mantra repeats in her head.
Words rolled off the tongues of men,
she repeats in the ears of others,
rolling over to maintain space.

Don't get attached.
Her words could easily offend.
She doesn't get attached,
keeps distance,
no longer yearns a companion.

Loved naively,
her ribs a railway track,
attached to unreciprocated potential.
Her heart's circuited agonising lessons,
clambered out of wells; she is wary.
She doesn't like to let people too close,
can't let them close;
she prefers her own company.
Another earring falls from a pair;
        they never stay for long.

Don't get attached, he'd say.
She repeats over the ears of men.

LAPIS LAZULI

TWO STEPS BACK

The barrier to all reason,
unlocked whirlwind,
self-destructive
pride, its own injury.

The monster of miscommunication,
volcanic ash, violent eruptions,
tsunami overpowers,
illogical compromiser
of life sentences.

NAT MUR*

there are worlds inside I try to escape
an unsatisfied mind hovers finding distractions
returning to a place of absence
pulled into the abyss
lanes where recollections are held in traffic
cars colliding
trucks pointing in the wrong direction
where there is absolute mayhem

into arteries clotted with pain
where movement seizes
gates closed
only visitors with lanyards allowed
a passer-by sneaks in
creeping into veins
claiming their home
stretching with a pitchfork
scraping insides
oblivious to the gasping bearer
every tug felt
every elbow blade
every careless foot
stomping instead of treading

an idle mind discovers lonely rooms
awaiting a visitor
to pause, linger
prodding the heart
bulldozing jammed doors

hauntings tumble
into the immaculate
courtyard.

---

* Take a seven-gram bottle of Nat Mur for a course of two weeks before
food. Store away from phone, in a cool dry place.

THE SCIENCE OF EIGHT LIMBS

Hands slip into gloves,
Velcro-fastened,
shoulder to chin,
hundred per cent focus,
the science of eight limbs,
stresses left outside.

Yoking back and forth,
elbows ready to strike
punching pads, kicking bags,
trauma and stifled blues released.
No space for a mind to drift,
focus on your breath.

Knee blades a shock to the ribcage,
may get kicked in the stomach,
resilience built for life's hurdles
– escaping a clench.

Pads pulled over shins,
heel to toe, ankle rotation.
Determined to develop strength.
Physically. Mentally. Spiritually.
Pushing past limits, advancing levels.
Resisting, succumbing to pain.

Kru drills, *Are you a master of yourself?*
Are you your own enemy?
Collective therapy,
no longer a victim,
a victor takes responsibility,
lessons transition,
commitment, consistency.

Stay present with yourself.

SATURN RETURN

THE HEN AND THE COCKEREL

Almost plucked the hairs out of my crown;
from a hen I'd turned into a cockerel,
though cockerels walk as though they are the majestic ones
when it's the hen who keeps the chickens alive.

She looks like a maid
whilst she stands beside her mate,
a shadow in his presence
for he makes all the noise,
waking the village for dawn prayer;
she sits by the hut as quiet as day.

I wanted to be more majestic, more fiery,
so I cut off my hair.
In the barber's chair I sat gladly,
as though I can only be a bold powerful woman
if I box myself into all that reflects masculine energy.

Placing my palm over my stomach,
concerned with insecurities
I'd birth if I fell pregnant.
I recognise my issues when I observe other women,
women more comfortable with their femininity.
When my hair was long,
I thought it made me look soft.
Is this what I project onto other women?
As though she is 'too girly'?
Too easy to impress,
valueless in this male-dominated society?
What influenced us to disbelieve
and misunderstand the woman?
I should be allowed to grow
my crown and attract.

Why is the cockerel the one who gets
the most pictures taken by the city
on the farmyard steps?
What are the influencing factors
of the way I see myself?

Am I to blame if a man's eyes focus on my chest?
Am I dirty 'cause every month
blood drips between my legs?
I feel almost embarrassed in the ladies' toilets
when the sound of peeling off my sanitary towel
can be heard by the woman in the cubicle on my left.

When did this occur,
this theft?

SIDEWALK

Shame made a home.
Boiled treacle flung, fear stuck to skin
eyes leering.

Scrutiny over decisions,
      the human condition,
      the openness of heart.

Shamed for everything resembling woman.

I kissed my palms,
abandoned her –

      I left shame in a black bin bag
      on the sidewalk.

SHE WITH SCALES

young woman
her fins unscathed
tail peacock turquoise
diving in deep
absorbing all below the shore
plunging in her own depths
a mermaid with unblinking eyes
scanning skies
between seaweed for insight
unafraid to wonder
allow life to unravel its hidden pearls
selective over whom to open her palms
wisdom gathered onto her expanding necklace
spiralling through life
choreographing her own dance
taking lessons to the children
awaiting her by the harbour
when she walks on her feet
tail safe in an upturned abandoned splintered boat
fastening gold trinket bell-laden bracelets
clasped draping her ankles
she strides with command and force
up hills and valleys
away from bustling cities
climbing with firm grip
plucking berries with her fingertips
antenna for lakes to pause by and recall
her fascinations
reflect on her assets
her fragilities, her soul's lessons, her fears
gazing at her reflection
separating strands of her hair
dishevelled, misplaced
astounded by her own controversial bipolarity
dancing on the tips of her toes
spinning a graceful frenzy
to freeze and drop to the floor
the weight of expectations denounced
weighs heavy on her subconscious
pondering who would bury her if she was disowned.

YONI VERSE

My yoni speaks in verses;
can't leave her out my couplets.

Hounded to disgrace her,
eradicate her many voices,

strangle her when she has urges.
My yoni's verse is drizzled in velvet,

draped around waists of continents,
hidden under dress ruffles.

She birthed nations;
her stories speak in volumes.

My yoni won't be silenced;
power comes from within her,

the transmitter of power,
creative energy releases through her gate.

She is life force,
a force to be reckoned with.

My yoni speaks in tongues,
never-ending riddles entering galaxies,

conception birthed between hips,
my yoni is where love sits.

BHAJI ON THE BEACH

They would go to the seaside,
Great Yarmouth, Skegness, Hunstanton,
samosas neatly packed, tennis rackets bagged,
squashed into the back of the car,
hitting the English countryside to make the journey.

Ladies in shalwar kameez, men in jeans
rolling trousers to their knees,
allowing the saline seawater to greet them,
kiss their feet before galloping back to its depths.

Family visits to the seaside,
pockets bulge with rock sweets,
2ps inserted into slots in the arcade,
children's eyebrows raised,
giggling through fingers,
reading on a stallholder's cap,
Squeeze me slowly, kiss me gently.
Wafer ice cream cones,
dohi-naa-baal candyfloss,
a baby tooth housed in a toffee-glazed Granny Smith,
mini buckets brimming with mollusc shells,
the sea's bones for Mum's cabinet.

As she gets older, she goes to the sea
in a bikini, no longer associated with family time.
Coconut oil lathered,
she bathes in the sun's medicine,
gulps novel pages, and writes,
comes home to herself when her mind feels fragile.

Warm ocean surrounds her shoulders,
waves sway her as she attempts to swim,
toes curled, nails scratched by marble,
her arms mimic strong swimmers.
She's the brown girl on the white beach,
toying hot granules of sand.

The sea breathes,
exhales and splutters,
she breathes out.

REBIRTH

burnt out, buried, bemused.
soil pounding down mercilessly
piercing her eyes,

blurring her vision and sight.
she chokes on earth forced
into her mouth,

charcoal stains her teeth,
focusing her breath.
breathing.

the taste of death no longer
lowering into her chest.
gradually rising from the dirt,

inhaling the scent of the cycle
of life in the earth.
burials have to take place

before it's time for rebirth.
lowering of coffins,
cremation of ashes.

ceremonies those
seemingly filled with life observe in a daze.
some feel every layer of the chapter,

some numb from their own wounds,
cut off from emotion,
the moon a cycle of time.

the pace of life and end,
perspective and angles from each crescent.
what does death look like in the desert?

where vultures pace,
parading overlooking
their next carcass.

soil underneath dry sand,
one day all going back into the land.
a nomad wandering,

searching for more life in the spiritual
imprint the Moors left behind.
seeking for meaning.

a new dawn with every season,
daily dissecting dues due.
observing the lotus blooming

amidst the muddy gloom.
growth forms in layers,
clearing space to make room.

journeys and cycles,
palms telling stories of wildness
reflecting veins in leaves.

nature's cure gallops in leaps
in woods, in forests,
in waves crashing against mountains.

hearts patient yet pounding,
the peering eyes of a newborn
blinded by light

catching sight of a midwife,
two legs inside a clock ticking,
anxious waiting, sticking hands.

PHOENIX RISES

Maybe us writers, poets and rhymers
are all just imaginative storytellers.
Sometimes we continue to tell our war stories
instead of coming from a place of healing,
intent that writing and reciting be our medicine,
rather than pain we vividly relive.

Let us let go together
today. Let's climb out our boxes,
watch from the angle of an eagle.
We manifest our perspective,
for every thought has power,
every word has an energy.
I'm going to take hold of the reins
for what the future holds,
what energies and intentions
I attract.

The few that have left
their energy inside my womb,
with or without consent,
their spirit trapped in the vessels of my body,
but today I summon these energies
I once let collide.

Free, fly away from me,
my mind, body and memory,
for you are
a weight I refuse to obsess over,
a pain I refuse to revisit.
I will shake you off like rain on a wet dog,
place down the rug in front of the fire.

I am for healing
before my addiction of replaying
and attracting more thunderstorms.
I'm not the metal pole no more,
standing in the street, waiting to be hit.

I'm the phoenix that rises from the ashes.

I'm the eagle that's learning
to keep my mouth shut and
understand the power of words.

I am strength for my sisters,
love for my brothers,
brothers who want to understand.

I'm learning my growl isn't enough,
so I become more gentle with my tone.
Light on the end of my   tongue
to kill the dark disease around us
we wallow in and recreate.

My tongue's a paintbrush;
I know its venom too.
Let's not glorify our darkness no more,
              how mad we can get,
              how many bones we're capable of breaking,
              how many phone calls I'd have to make
to hug my ego better when disrespected.

I will leave you behind like I did
when I got on that plane,
the way I've left people behind I love,
land, memories and serenity.

This is my mantra
every time someone I let close
fails to appreciate me
or trespasses, their ego
assuming some kind of authority.

I will rise from the ashes and make a bonfire.

Where I burn every encounter
which attempted to make me doubt myself,

to shake me,
to challenge my confidence.

I embrace growth and rise
from the ashes.
I am a phoenix.

I can only grow stronger, never weaker.
I straighten my feathers, I take off.

ACKNOWLEDGEMENTS

Every soul we meet, every story we've heard, every interaction we've had impacts us. Love to everyone who has contributed to awakening a deeper understanding of the beauty and ills in this world inside me. Thank you for taking the time to read my collection, and to everyone who has ever given me a platform, and empowered me with encouragement.

Special thanks to Anthony Anaxagorou and Afshan D'souza-Lodhi for mentoring me through the editing process, challenging and improving me as a writer. Thank you, Ramon Gazhang, RGZGcreative, for the photography and designing the cover. Shagufta K Iqbal and JJ Bola, I appreciate your consistent support and demands for a collection from me. Thank you Milli Bhatia for supporting directing performance and Sami El-Enany for composing music for the launch of this collection. Thank you Benjamin Zephaniah, Amrit Wilson, Caleb Femi, Rodney P and Samia Malik for the support. Love to everyone at Burning Eye Books and Arts Council England for supporting my debut.

Special thanks to my therapist Muku; without your support the headspace for this collection would not have been possible. Thank you Mum, for always ensuring my mind was nurtured and supporting my love for storytelling and writing. I have always admired and drawn strength from your resilient spirit. Thank you, Papa, for not putting glass ceilings over my head.

Many talented writers raised in working-class ethnic 'minority' communities do not get the support to reach their dreams due to lack of resources, representation or encouragement. I hope this collection inspires others to embrace their journey and preferred art with both hands, to speak their truth unapologetically.

GLOSSARY

Adhaan: the Muslim call to prayer.

Babi: Gujarati baby word for chapatti.

Baaji: Gujarati word for grandfather.

Bhaji: Indian cuisine. A small flat cake or ball of vegetables with
spices, fried in batter.

Bhel puri: an Indian dish of puffed rice, onions, spices and hot
chutney.

Chapatti: Indian cuisine. A thin pancake of unleavened wholemeal
bread cooked on a griddle.

Dholak: a South Asian two-headed hand drum, used in North
India.

Dohi-naa-baal: old woman's hair. Gujarati description for
candyfloss.

Haraam: prohibited and forbidden in Islamic law.

Innit: isn't it.

Istikhara: a prayer recited by Muslims when in need of guidance
on an issue in their life, to obtain clarity in their dreams.

Jabal Al-Zaytoun: Mount of Olives in Jerusalem.

Jeera: cumin seeds.

Jugalbandhi: a performance in Indian classical music. 'Entwined
twins'. The duet can be either vocal or instrumental.

Kru: Thai word for teacher. A Muay Thai Kru is a master of Muay
Thai.

Khuri kitchari: Gujarati rice dish, made with a yoghurt-based
curry made of buttermilk, plain yoghurt, fresh coriander,
onion and curry leaves.

Lapis lazuli: deep blue metamorphic rock used as a semi-precious
stone, from the northern province of Afghanistan. It
symbolises royalty, honour, power, spirit and vision. A
stone beneficial for the throat chakra and communication.

Maa: mother / grandmother.

Manzil: palace.

Nat Mur: a homeopathic remedy.

Tawa: a griddle iron flat pan South Asians use to make chapatti
on

Pikin: Sierra Leonean Krio word for child.

Salone: Sierra Leone. Also a patriotic name for Sierra Leoneans.

Shukra: Sanskrit word that means 'lucid, clear and bright'. In medieval mythology and Hindu astrology, the term refers to the planet Venus.

Sitafal: custard apple.

Yoni: Sanskrit word interpreted to literally mean the womb and female organs. 'The source of all life' or 'sacred space'.

Zaatar: Arabic word for thyme.